PRAYING 101
for

WOMEN

By

Dottie Randazzo

Praying 101 *for* WOMEN

by
Dottie Randazzo

Creative Dreaming
6433 Topanga Cyn. Blvd.
120
Woodland Hills, CA 91303

All rights reserved. No part of this book may be reproduced or transmitted in any form or by any means, electronic or mechanical, including photocopying, recording or by any information storage and retrieval system, without permission from the author, except for the inclusion of brief quotations in a review.

Copyright © 2007 by Dottie Randazzo

ISBN 978-0-6151-5521-0

God has not always answered my prayers. If he had, I would have married the wrong man – several times.

Ruth Bell Graham

By Dottie Randazzo

Praying 101 for Spiritual Enlightenment
Praying 101 for Kids & Teens
Praying 101 for Men
Praying 101 for Women
Praying 101 for Parents

Introduction

I realized a long time ago that most of us think that our prayers are not heard because we aren't getting what we want. But it's not that our prayers aren't heard; it's all in the asking. A few years ago, when a friend told me that she wanted something. I asked her if she'd said a prayer for it. She told me she didn't know how to pray.

As a child I attended both Baptist and Lutheran schools where I was taught how to memorize a few really good prayers, such as the Lord's Prayer. I was never really taught how to pray.

I know how to pray. I am not sure how I learned, but I did. All you have to do is ask my sister and she will tell you. She has often said I have a direct line to the heavens!

This book will teach you how to pray. It is your basic prayer book. I have designed a prayer for many aspects of your life. Once you have learned the key ingredients to praying you will have the tools to customize your own prayers. So let's flip the page and begin to solve the mystery of prayer.

Commonly Asked Questions

Do I need to know any special language to pray?

You do not need to know any special language. Your language and words will be understood.

Who do I pray to?

It does not matter whether you are praying to God. Our Father, The Masters of the Universe, or whomever, your prayer will be heard. Pray to the One that you believe in.

When and where should I pray?

Praying can be done anytime and anywhere. If you want to say your prayer in the morning, then that is when you should say it. If you want to say your prayer while taking a bath or shower, then that's when you should.

Do I have to kneel down or say my prayer out loud?

No kneeling needed. You can stand, lie down or even be getting your nails done. It doesn't matter; your prayer will be heard. Your prayer does not need to be said out loud.

How do I pray?

To pray you use the little voice in your head. The same one that you hear when someone walks into the room with a weird hairdo and you hear in your head, *what was she thinking with that hair?* That's the same voice that you are going to say your prayer with. Those same voices in your head that you hear say, *I did well* or *I should not have done that*. It is almost like talking to yourself except you do it in your head. Say your prayer just like you are writing a letter; begin with "Dear____." And always end your prayer with thanks. Thanks for listening, thanks for caring, thanks for looking out for me. Gratitude goes a long way in life.

If I don't get what I am asking for, does that mean my prayer was not heard?

Not getting what you want absolutely does not mean that your prayer was not heard. We always get what we want. We may not get it when we want it. We get it when we are supposed to.

> When the gods choose to punish us, they merely answer our prayers.
>
> **Oscar Wilde**

Very Important Things You Should Know

Everything happens for a reason. . If something bad happens to you, you need to look at the experience and see what you were supposed to learn from it. For example, you have an argument with a friend. You sit down and write a nasty, but what you believe to be true, letter telling your friend what you really think. You send the letter and a few days later you hear from your friend. As you talk to your friend, you think that she has gotten the letter and you have ironed out the misunderstanding between the two of you. A few days later the letter has been returned to you and your friend never received it. You realize that if your friend had gotten your letter, the friendship would not have been repairable. You are so thankful that your friend did not get the letter. It's like the Masters of the Universe were looking out for your friendship.

Everything happens exactly when it is supposed to. This might not be when you want it to happen. For example, let's say that you saw a dress that you really feel in love with, but your size was not available. You are upset and think that life's just not fair. You walk into another store and find a dress that is ten times better than the last one you saw that you wanted. If you take the time to look back, you would realize, it was a blessing that the dress you first saw was not available in your size.

You are doing in your life exactly what you are supposed to be doing at this exact moment. Every single moment in your life is very important and every single moment in your life affects the next moment in your life. Every person that you meet has a reason to be in your life, even if just for a brief moment. Some people come into our lives for a reason and some for a season.

Enjoy your life. You must learn to enjoy your life. Eating your breakfast in the morning is part of your life. Don't sit down and eat it fast while you are thinking of something else. This is a very bad habit to start. When you are older it will take you twice as long to fix the bad habit. Every single day is a very important day in your life. It is a day that you will never get to relive. Learn to appreciate every moment and don't take them for granted.

Pray for wisdom. Wisdom is smarts, answers, solutions and brainpower. When you ask for wisdom you ask to be aware of the right answers. Wisdom allows you to see answers when they enter your life. For example, you want to know if you should stay in a relationship or not. Like everything else, it has its good side and its bad side. The good is really really good and the bad is really really bad. So you are confused and don't know what to do. Pray for a sign. Pray for the wisdom to make the right decision. I said this prayer once and 7 days after I said the prayer I caught my husband with another woman. Yes, I was crushed. But I did after all, get an answer to my prayer. I got that sign that I should close that chapter in my life and end the relationship. Sometimes we get answers but they don't always come to us the way we think that they should and therefore we don't see the answer. We miss them because we are looking for them to be delivered our way. Answers are delivered the way that they are suppose to be delivered, not necessarily the way that we want them delivered.

Believe that your prayers are heard and will be answered. Why pray if you don't have any faith. The bible says that faith the size of a mustard seed can move a mountain. Like Wow!

Have you ever seen a mustard seed? It's tiny. Don't try praying to test the system. It doesn't work. The system does not need to be tested by you.

Prayer, like radium, is a luminous and self-generating form of energy.

Alexis Carrel

Prayer for Good Health

Dear Lord,

I pray for the wisdom to maintain/obtain a good strong healthy body. I pray for the awareness that my body is a reflection of your creation and it is perfect in every way. Thank you for taking care of me.

Prayer to End an Abusive Relationship

Dear God,

I pray for the strength, courage and wisdom to move beyond the abusive relationship I am in. I pray for the courage to stand up for my beliefs and myself. I pray for the strength not to be bullied into a bad situation just to be accepted. I pray for the wisdom to be able to see the lesson in this situation and to grow from it in a positive way. Thank you for blessing me.

Prayer to Relieve Menopause Symptoms

Dear Masters of the Universe,

I pray for the wisdom to make the correct choices regarding my health. I pray that I will be guided towards the best treatment for me. I pray that you remove any feelings of insecurity that I possess. Thank you for taking care of me.

Prayer for The Health of Someone Else

Dear Goddess,

I pray and ask you to bless my friend/relative with good health. I pray that they will have the wisdom to see and make the correct choices for their health. I pray that you remove any feelings of insecurity that they may possess. Thank you for listening to me.

Prayer for Better Relationships

(With Parents, Siblings, Spouses and/or Children)

Dear Higher Power,

I pray for the wisdom to help me to have a better relationship with those that I love. I pray for the wisdom to understand them. I pray that they have the wisdom to understand me. Thank you for listening to me.

Prayer for Safety in Travels or Vacations

Dear Father,

I pray for the wisdom to make the correct choices regarding my safety and the safety of others while traveling and/or on vacation. Thank you for taking care of me.

Prayer to Overcome Feelings of Loneliness

Dear Lord,

I pray for the wisdom and strength to remove the loneliness that I feel inside. I pray that you will send someone into my life to have fun and share my life with. I pray that you remove any feelings of insecurity that I possess. I pray for the wisdom to be able to see the lesson in this situation and to grow from it in a positive way. I pray for the wisdom to love my body. I pray for the awareness that my body is a reflection of your creation and it is perfect in every way. I pray that you remove any feelings of insecurity that I possess. Thank you for blessing me.

Prayer for Intuition

Dear God,

I pray for the wisdom to learn how to use my intuition. I pray for the wisdom to be able to see the correct choices in life. Thank you for listening to me.

Prayer Because I am too Thin or Anorexic

Dear Masters of the Universe,

I pray for the wisdom to be able to identify bad eating habits from healthy ones. I pray that others will not judge me because of my weight and that they will see me for the great person that I am in on the inside. I pray for the wisdom to be able to see the lesson(s) in this situation and to grow from it in a positive way. I pray for the wisdom to love my body. I pray for the awareness that my body is a reflection of your creation and it is perfect in every way. I pray for good health. I pray that you remove any feelings of insecurity that I possess. Thank you for taking care of me.

Prayer for Better Finances

Dear Goddess,

I pray for the wisdom to understand my finances better. I pray for the strength and the courage not to waste money. I pray for the wisdom to see the correct choices for my finances. Thank you for blessing me.

Prayer to Overcome Hate and Anxiety

Dear Higher Power,

I pray for the wisdom, courage and strength to remove the hate that I feel for another individual. I pray for the wisdom to remove all anxiety that I am suffering from. I pray for the wisdom to replace those feelings of hate and anxiety with feelings of compassion and understanding. I pray for the courage to stand up for my beliefs and myself. I pray for the strength not to be bullied into a bad situation just to fit in. I pray for the wisdom to be able to see the lesson in this situation and to grow from it in a positive way. I pray that you remove any feelings of insecurity that I possess. Thank you for taking care of me.

Prayer for Fertility/Adoption

Dear Father,

I pray for the wisdom to be able to see the correct choices, be it fertility treatment or adoption. I pray for my health and the health and the health of my future baby. I pray that you remove any insecurity that I possess. Thank you for blessing me.

Prayer for Better Memory

Dear Lord,

I pray for the wisdom to have a better memory. I pray that you remove any feelings of insecurity that I possess. Thank you for listening to me.

Prayer to Overcome Addictions
(Gambling, Anorexia, Bulimia, Drugs, Alcohol, Smoking, Shopping)

Dear God,

I pray for the wisdom, strength and courage to recognize things in my life that will help me overcome my addiction(s). I pray for the wisdom to make the correct choices and to stand up for my beliefs and myself. I pray for the courage not to be bullied into a bad situation just to fit in. I pray for the wisdom to love my body. I pray for the awareness that my body is a reflection of your creation and it is perfect in every way. I pray that you remove any feelings of insecurity that I possess. Thank you for listening to me.

Prayer to Tell the Truth and Not Lie

Dear Masters of the Universe,

I pray for the wisdom, strength and courage to tell the truth and not lie. I pray that I will have the courage to stand up for my beliefs and myself. I pray for the strength not to be bullied into a bad situation just to fit in. Thank you for blessing me.

Prayer for Divorced Parents

Dear Goddess,

I pray that you will bless both of my parents and guide them with the wisdom to see and make the correct choices regarding our family. I pray that you remove any hurt, hate or unhealthy feelings from my family. I pray that you bless us with an abundance of understanding. I pray for the wisdom to be able to see the lesson in this situation and to grow from it in a positive way. I pray that you remove any feelings of insecurity that I possess. Thank you for taking care of me.

Prayer for Dealing with the Death of a Loved One

Dear Higher Power,

I pray that my loved one is safe, taken care of, happy and free of any pain or illness. I pray for the strength and courage to go on with my life. I pray for the wisdom to understand this loss. I pray for the wisdom and strength not to let my emotions disable me. I pray that you remove any pain or loneliness that I feel in my heart. Thank you for taking care of me.

Prayer for Love

Dear Father,

I pray for the wisdom to love myself and others unconditionally. I pray for the wisdom to love all that you created and see the good in it. Thank you for blessing me.

Prayer to Be True to Yourself

Dear Lord,

I pray for the courage to stand up for my beliefs and myself. I pray for the strength not to be bullied into a bad situation just to fit in. I pray for the wisdom to love my body. Thank you for looking out for me.

Prayer to Learn Life's Purpose

Dear God,

I pray for the wisdom to learn my life's purpose. I pray that my intuition will guide me in the right direction. I pray that I will see the correct choices. I pray for the wisdom to remove any anxiety or confusion. I pray for confidence in my abilities. Thank you for taking care of me.

Prayer to Overcome Panic Attacks

Dear Masters of the Universe,

I pray for the wisdom, strength and courage to overcome my panic attacks. I pray for the wisdom to be able to see the lesson in this situation and to grow from it in a positive way. I pray for the wisdom to love my body. I pray for the awareness that my body is a reflection of your creation and it is perfect in every way. I pray that you remove any feelings of insecurity that I possess. Thank you for taking care of me.

Prayer for Self-Esteem and Self-Worth

Dear Goddess,

I pray that you bless me with an abundance of self-esteem and self-worth. I pray for the wisdom to be able to distinguish self-destructive behavior from productive, healthy behavior. I pray that I never forget my self-worth. I pray for the strength and courage to stand up for my beliefs and myself. I pray for the courage not to be bullied into a bad situation just to fit in. I pray for the wisdom to love my body. I pray for the awareness that my body is a reflection of your creation and it is perfect in every way. Thank you for listening to me.

Prayer for Pregnancy

Dear Higher Power,

I pray for the wisdom to make the correct choices. I pray for my health and the health of my baby. I pray for the strength and courage to stand up for my beliefs and not to be bullied into a bad situation just to fit in. I pray for the wisdom to be able to see the lesson in this situation and to grow from it in a positive way. I pray for the wisdom to love my body. I pray for the awareness that my body is a reflection of your creation and it is perfect in every way. I pray that you remove any feelings of insecurity that I possess. Thank you for listening to me.

Prayer for Good Judgment

Dear Father,

I pray for the wisdom to make the correct choices and to exercise good judgment in every area of my life. Thank you for blessing me.

Prayer for Mental Strength and Courage

Dear Lord,

I pray for mental strength and courage. I pray for the wisdom to make the correct choices and to stand up for my beliefs and myself. I pray for the strength not to be bullied into a bad situation just to fit in. I pray that you remove any feelings of insecurity that I possess. Thank you for listening to me.

Prayer for Aging Gracefully

Dear God,

I pray that you bless me with self-love. I pray for the wisdom to see and make the correct choices in my life. I pray for the wisdom to love my body. I pray for the awareness that my body is a reflection of your creation and it is perfect in every way. I pray that you remove any feelings of insecurity that I possess. Thank you for listening to me.

Prayer to Get the Message

Dear Masters of the Universe,

I pray for the wisdom to learn what I am suppose to learn during my time here on earth. I pray that I will be guided and protected as I walk through life. I pray for the wisdom to see the daily miracles that are so graciously sprinkled in my life. Thank you for taking care of me.

Prayer for Marriage, Commitment, Relationship and/or Companionship

Dear Goddess,

I pray that you bless me with a wonderful mate. I pray for the wisdom to see and make the correct choices. I pray that you protect me from evil people. I pray for the strength and the courage to have the patience for the right person to come into my life. I pray that you remove any feelings of insecurity that I possess. Thank you for listening to me.

Prayer to Embrace Simplicity

Dear Higher Power,

I pray for the wisdom to remember that true simplicity is a conscious life choice which illuminates our life within. I pray for the strength and courage to be liberated from the bondage and burden of extravagance and excess. I pray for the wisdom to see the simple gifts that each and every day offers us. Thank you for listening to me.

Prayer for the Kindness of Strangers

Dear Father,

I pray for the wisdom to become consciously aware of my encounters with strangers. I pray for the wisdom to recognize an angelic meeting. I pray that you remove the uncomfortable feelings that I have when I don't ask for assistance from others. I pray for the wisdom to remove the feeling that a little help is too much to ask for. I pray for the wisdom to be kind to strangers and to let strangers be kind to me. I pray for comfort and compassion. Thank you for listening to me.

Prayer for the Fear of Success

Dear Lord,

I pray for the wisdom, strength, courage to leave my comfort zone and predictable life. I pray for the wisdom to welcome change. I pray for the wisdom to eliminate the uncomfortable feelings I have associated with change. I pray for the wisdom to achieve one challenge at a time. I am thankful for my accomplishments.

Prayer to Take Action

Dear God,

I pray for the wisdom, strength and courage to take action. I pray for the wisdom, strength and courage to move forward and stop procrastinating. I pray for the wisdom to be consciously aware that there are no accidents. I pray for the wisdom to be consciously aware that mistakes will happen for me to learn from. I pray for your guidance. Thank you for listening to me.

Prayer for Creativity

Dear Masters of the Universe,

I pray for creativity in my project. I pray for patience to participate in the creative process. I pray for the wisdom to recognize the creative signs that are being shown to me. I pray for enthusiasm and motivation. I pray for the strength to overcome procrastination. Thank you for taking care of me.

Prayer for Employment

Dear Goddess,

I pray for the wisdom to find employment. I pray for the wisdom to see the correct choices for me. I pray for the wisdom to learn what skills, training and/or education I need to make me more employable. I pray for you to remove any insecurity that I possess. I pray for the wisdom to see the lesson in this situation and to grow from it in a positive way. I pray for the wisdom to remove any anxiety or confusion. I pray for confidence in my abilities. I pray for enthusiasm and motivation. I pray for the strength to overcome procrastination. Thank you for blessing me.

Prayer for Making Dreams Come True

Dear Higher Power,

Thank you for giving me the wisdom, strength and creativity to make all my dreams come true.

Prayer to Overcome PMS

Dear Father,

I pray for the wisdom, strength and courage to realize that my hormones are intensified at this time in my life. I pray for the wisdom, strength and courage to be able to control my thoughts. I pray for the strength to not say or do anything irrational that will hurt or harm my relationships. I pray for peaceful and tranquil feelings. Thank you for caring about me.

Prayer to Be the Woman You Were Meant to Be

Dear Lord,

I pray for the wisdom and strength to stop being the woman I think I am suppose to be and to be the woman I was meant to be. I pray for the strength to remove the feelings I feel when I look in the mirror and don't recognize myself. I pray for the strength to turn away from the world and to listen to my heart. Thank you for blessing me.

Prayer for Kicking the Fear Habit

(Elevators, Automobiles, Flying and Animals)

Dear God,

I pray for the wisdom, strength and courage to keep my mind at peace. I pray for the wisdom, strength and courage to be consciously aware that you are protecting me. I pray that you remove any anxieties that I am feeling. I pray for the wisdom, strength and courage to remove all feelings of fear that I am exhibiting. I pray for peace and contentment. Thank you for taking care of me.

Prayer to Overcome Sabotaging Behavior

Dear Masters of the Universe,

I pray for the wisdom, strength and courage to recognize sabotaging behavior. I pray for the wisdom, strength and courage to remove the sabotaging behavior from my life. I pray for the wisdom, strength and courage to replace the sabotaging behavior with healthy, productive behavior. Thank you for blessing me.

Prayer to Reinvent Yourself

Dear Goddess,

I pray for the wisdom to reinvent myself. I pray for the wisdom, strength and courage to stop living the life I think that I am suppose to live. I pray for the wisdom, strength and courage not to care about living up to someone else's expectations. I pray for the wisdom, strength and courage to wake up each morning and live my life exactly the way that I want to live it. I pray for the wisdom to remember that I am the only one who is responsible for my happiness and my successes. I pray for the will power and enthusiasm to create a passionate life. Thank you for blessing me.

Prayer to Eliminate Negative Relationships

Dear Higher Power,

I pray for the wisdom, strength and courage to let go of the negative attachments that I have to friends and relatives who damage my relationships. I pray that you will bless them and guide them to a life of peace and fulfillment. Thank you for listening to me.

Prayer to Rise to the Occasion

Dear Father,

I thank you for the wisdom to cope with my situation. I thank you for the wisdom to rise to the occasion and do whatever needs to be done. I thank you for giving me the strength and courage to handle life.

Prayer to Overcome Insomnia

Dear Lord,

I pray that you will free my mind of all worry. I pray for the wisdom to release all tension in my body. I pray for the strength and courage to know that my life is exactly as it should be at every given moment. I pray for relaxation and a peaceful night of sleep. Thank you for listening to me.

Prayer for More Energy and Higher Metabolism

Dear God,

I pray that you bless me with the wisdom, strength and courage to do the things in my life that will give me more energy and increase my metabolism. I pray for the wisdom, strength and courage to make the correct choices regarding my health. Thank you for loving me.

Prayer for Your Inner Child

Dear Masters of the Universe,

I pray for the wisdom, strength and courage to identify my inner child. I pray for the wisdom, strength and courage to nurture and love my inner child. I pray for the wisdom, strength and courage to realize that I need my inner child and it is a significant part of my being. Thank you for loving me.

Prayer to Overcome Mood Swings

Dear Goddess,

I pray for the wisdom to be able to identify my mood swings. I pray for the wisdom, strength and courage to know that making a decision while having a mood swing may not be in the best interest of me, my family or anyone else I come in contact with. I pray that I have the wisdom to relax and know that this too shall pass. I pray that others do not judge me by my mood swings and see me for the great person that I am. I pray that you remove any feelings of insecurity that I possess. Thank you for blessing to me.

Prayer for A Wonderful Wedding

Dear Higher Power,

I pray for my wedding day to be blessed. I pray for the safety and happiness of everyone who attends my wedding. I pray for patience on this day. I pray that you remove any insecurity that I may possess. I pray that if things don't happen the way I planned, I will have the wisdom to see and learn the lesson(s) necessary. Thank you for listening to me.

Prayer to Be a Good Step-Mother

Dear Father,

I pray for the wisdom, strength and courage to be a good step-mother. I pray for the wisdom to be able to identify opportunities which will benefit my family. I pray for patience in dealing with my family. I pray for the strength and courage to stand up for my beliefs and not to be bullied into a situation to fit in. I pray that my family is blessed with unconditional love. I pray that my family has the wisdom to see and identify unconditional love. I pray that my family has the courage to love each other unconditionally. Thank you for blessing me.

Prayer to Have a Different Perception

Dear Lord,

I pray for the wisdom to have a different perception. I pray for the strength and courage to see another point of view. Thank you for listening to me.

Prayer for Radiant Health

Dear God,

I pray for radiant health. I pray for the wisdom to be aware of what radiant health is. I pray that you remove any negative feelings that I may possess regarding my health. Thank you for blessing me.

Prayer to Stick with a Diet

Dear Masters of the Universe,

I pray for the wisdom, strength and courage to be able to stay on my diet. I pray for the wisdom to be aware of the benefits, every minute of every day, for staying on my diet. I pray that I will have the strength and courage to be able to turn away from temptation. I pray for the wisdom to love my body. I pray for the awareness that my body is a reflection of your creation and it is perfect in every way. I pray that you remove any feelings of insecurity that I possess. Thank you for taking care of me.

Prayer to Be a Stay at Home Mom

Dear Goddess,

I pray for the wisdom to see opportunities which will allow me to be a stay at home mom. I pray for the strength and courage to stand up for my beliefs and to not be bullied into a situation just to fit in. Thank you for listening to me.

Prayer to Stay Together for Our Children

Dear Higher Power,

I pray for the wisdom, strength and courage to see opportunities that will allow me to work through my current problems so that my family can stay together. I pray for the strength and courage to stand up for my beliefs and not to be bullied into a situation to fit in. I pray that my family is blessed with unconditional love. I pray that my family has the wisdom to see and identify unconditional love. I pray that my family has the courage to love each other unconditionally. Thank you for taking care of us.

Prayer for Cooking

Dear Father,

I pray for the wisdom to be aware that my cooking serves the basic needs of food, security and love. I pray for the wisdom to be aware that we cannot think of one without the other. Thank you for blessing me.

Prayer for Laughter

Dear Lord,

I pray for the wisdom to live my life with a light heart. I pray for the wisdom to be aware that laughter is good for the soul and healing. I pray for the strength and courage not to take life so seriously. Thank you for listening to me.

Prayer for The Technically Challenged

Dear God,

I pray that you remove any feelings that I have about being technically challenged. I pray for the wisdom to be aware of what I can do to become less technically challenged. I pray that you remove any insecurity that I may possess. Thank you for loving me.

Prayer to Overcome Fatigue

Dear Masters of the Universe,

I pray for the wisdom to be aware that fatigue is a sign that I should be taking better care of myself. I pray for the wisdom and awareness to understand that I am not my best when I am fatigued. Thank you for blessing me.

Prayer to Recover from a Major Illness

Dear Goddess,

I pray for a speedy recovery. I pray for the wisdom to be aware of the lessons necessary to be learned from this situation. I pray that you remove any insecurity that I possess. Thank you for blessing me.

Prayer for Learning to Create Boundaries

Dear Higher Power,

I pray for the wisdom to create boundaries to protect, nurture and care for all that is important to me. I pray for the strength and courage to speak up. Thank you for listening to me.

Prayer to Create Your Day

Dear Father,

I pray for the wisdom to be aware that upon waking up each morning I possess the power to create my day. I pray for the strength and courage to create a fabulous magnificent day. Thank you for loving me.

Prayer to Overcome Confusion

Dear Lord,

I am confused and do not know what decision is the correct decision. I pray for the wisdom to be able to identify which decision is the correct decision for me. I pray for the courage to stand up for my beliefs and myself. I pray for the strength not to be bullied into a bad situation just to fit in. I pray for the wisdom to be able to see the lesson in this situation and to grow from it in a positive way. Thank you for taking care of me.

Prayer for a New School or New Job

Dear God,

I pray that you will remove any fear or anxiety from me about attending my new school or new job. I pray that you will protect me from all harm and evil people. I pray for the wisdom to make new friends and see enemies. I pray for the courage to stand up for my beliefs and myself and not to be bullied into a bad situation just to fit in. I pray for the wisdom to learn what is being taught to me. I pray that you remove any feelings of insecurity that I possess. Thank you for taking care of me.

Prayer to Forgive Someone

Dear Masters of the Universe,

I pray for the wisdom, strength, courage and compassion to forgive the individual who I feel has betrayed me. I pray for the wisdom to see and make the correct choices in this situation. I pray for the courage to stand up for my beliefs and not to be bullied into a bad situation just to fit in. I pray for the wisdom to be able to see the lesson in this situation and to grow from it in a positive way. Thank you for blessing me.

Prayer for Sports

Dear Goddess,

I pray for wisdom to perfect my skills and talents regarding my favorite sports. I pray for the wisdom to be aware of opportunities to become better at my favorite sport. I pray for my safety and the safety of others while I am participating in my favorite sports. I pray that you remove any feelings of insecurity that I possess. Thank you for blessing me.

Prayer for New Home and Neighborhood

Dear Higher Power,

I pray that you will bless our new home and neighborhood. I pray for the safety of my family in our new home and neighborhood. I pray that you will bless us with an abundance of happy memories in our new home and neighborhood. I pray that you remove any feelings of insecurity that I possess. Thank you for taking care of us.

Prayer Wisdom Regarding My Sexuality

Dear Father,

I pray for the wisdom to see and make the correct choices regarding my sexuality. I pray for the strength and courage to stand up for my beliefs and myself. I pray for the strength not to be bullied into a bad situation just to fit in. I pray that others will see me for the person that I am on the inside and not judge me by my sexual preferences. I pray for the wisdom to love my body. I pray that you protect me from evil. I pray for the awareness that my body is a reflection of your creation and it is perfect in every way. I pray that you remove any feelings of insecurity that I possess. Thank you for looking out for me.

Prayer for Hobbies

Dear Lord,

I pray for the wisdom to perfect my skills and talents regarding my hobby or hobbies. I pray for the wisdom to be aware of the opportunities to become better at my hobby or hobbies. I pray for my safety and the safety of others while I am participating in my hobby or hobbies. I pray that you remove any feelings of insecurity that I possess. Thank you for listening.

Prayer to Live in the Moment

Dear God,

I pray for the wisdom to be aware each and every day of my special life. I pray for the wisdom to not take anything for granted and to be gracious of the gift of life. Thank you for blessing me.

Prayer for Dealing with a Spoiled Child

Dear Masters of the Universe,

I pray for the wisdom to see opportunities that are available for me to help my spoiled child. I pray for patience and the patience of my family when dealing with this child. I pray for the strength and courage to stand up for myself and my beliefs and not to be bullied into a bad situation. I pray for the safety of my child and other children my child comes in contact with. Thank you for taking care of us.

Prayer for The Extraordinary

Dear Goddess,

I pray for the wisdom to be aware of the extraordinary that is in everything ordinary. Thank you for blessing me.

Prayer to Exercise Regularly

Dear Higher Power,

I pray for the wisdom, strength and courage to exercise regularly. I pray for the wisdom to be able to recognize the benefits. I pray for the wisdom to love my body. I pray for the awareness that my body is a reflection of your creation and it is perfect in every way. I pray that you remove any feelings of insecurity I possess. Thank you for blessing me.

Prayer to Speak Up

Dear Father,

I pray for the wisdom, courage and strength to speak up for myself. I pray for the wisdom to be able to recognize the benefits of speaking up for myself. I pray for strength and courage to stand up for myself and my beliefs and not to be bullied into any situation just to fit in. I pray that you remove any feelings of insecurity that I may possess. Thank you for taking care of me.

Prayer for Inspiration

Dear Lord,

I pray for the wisdom and awareness to see inspiration all around me. Thank you for listening to me.

Prayer to Love my Body

Dear God,

I pray for the wisdom, strength and courage to love my body. I pray for the strength and courage to stand up for my beliefs and myself and not to be bullied into a bad situation just to fit in. I pray for the awareness that my body is a reflection of your creation and it is perfect in every way. I pray that you remove any feelings of insecurity that I possess. Thank you for looking out for me.

Prayer for Selflessness

Dear Masters of the Universe,

I pray for the wisdom to be selfless. I pray that I will be able to help others when needed and not expect anything from them. I pray for the wisdom to remember that the payback for selflessness is your blessings in my life. I pray that I am able to care for others from the goodness of my heart. I pray that I have the strength and courage to stand up for my beliefs and myself. I pray for the strength not to be bullied into a bad situation just to fit in. Thank you for listening to me.

Prayer for The Truth

Dear Goddess,

I pray for the wisdom to be aware of the truth. I pray for the strength and courage to stand up for my beliefs. I pray for the wisdom to see the benefit in the truth. I pray for the strength and courage not to be bullied into a situation just to fit in. Thank you for blessing me.

Prayer for a Good Job Review

Dear Father,

I pray that I receive a good job review. I pray that if I do not receive a good job review that I will have the wisdom to be aware of the lessons to be learned. I pray that you remove any insecurity that I may possess. Thank you for blessing me.

Prayer for Seeing Miracles

Dear Lord,

I pray for the wisdom to be aware of the miracles that are sprinkled in my life every day. Thank you for blessing me.

My Personalized Prayers

PRAYER FOR/TO

Aging Gracefully.	26
A Wonderful Wedding . . .	47
Because I am too Thin or Anorexic . .	..9
Be a Good Step-Mother . . .	48
Be a Stay at Home Mom . . .	52
Be the Woman You Were Meant to Be .	37
Better Finances	10
Better Memory	13
Better Relationships	..5
Be True to Yourself	19
Cooking	54
Create Your Day	60
Creativity	33
Dealing with a Spoiled Child. . .	69
Dealing with the Death of a Loved One .	17
Divorced Parents	16
Eliminate Negative Relationships . .	41
Embrace Simplicity	29
Employment	34
End an Abusive Relationship . .	..2
Exercise Regularly	71

Fear of Success	31
Fertility/Adoption	12
Forgive Someone.	63
Get the Message	27
Good Health	..1
Good Job Review	77
Good Judgment	24
Have a Different Perception	49
Hobbies	67
Inspiration	73
Intuition	..8
Kicking the Fear Habit	38
Kindness of Strangers	30
Laughter	55
Learning to Create Boundaries	59
Learn Life's Purpose	20
Live in the Moment	68
Love	18
Love my Body	74
Making Dreams Come True	35
Marriage, Commitment, Relationship and/or Companionship	28
Mental Strength and Courage	25

More Energy and Higher Metabolism	44
New Home and Neighborhood	65
New School or New Job	62
Overcome Addictions	14
Overcome Confusion	61
Overcome Fatigue	57
Overcome Feelings of Loneliness	..7
Overcome Hate and Anxiety	11
Overcome Insomnia	43
Overcome Mood Swings	46
Overcome Panic Attacks	21
Overcome PMS	36
Overcome Sabotaging Behavior	39
Pregnancy	23
Radiant Health	50
Recover from a Major Illness	58
Reinvent Yourself	40
Relieve Menopause Symptoms	..3
Rise to the Occasion	43
Safety in Travels or Vacations	..6
Seeing Miracles	78
Self-Esteem and Self-Worth	22
Selflessness	75

Speaking Up 72

Sports 64

Stay Together for Our Children . . 53

Stick with a Diet 51

Take Action 32

Tell the Truth and Not Lie . . . 15

The Extraordinary 70

The Health of Someone Else 4

The Technically Challenged . . . 56

The Truth 76

Wisdom Regarding My Sexuality . . 66

Your Inner Child . . . 45

www.ingramcontent.com/pod-product-compliance
Lightning Source LLC
Chambersburg PA
CBHW032018040426
42448CB00006B/658